How To Master
Microsoft OneNote 2013

Top 10 OneNote Hacks & Secrets For Beginners

The Blokehead

TABLE OF CONTENTS

Get Notice of Our New Releases Here!

http://clika.pe/l/10263/27048/

ABOUT US

The Blokehead is an extensive series of instructional/how to books which are intended to present quick and easy to use guides for readers new to the various topics covered.

The Series is divided into the following sub-series:

1. The Blokehead Success Series

2. The Blokehead Journals

3. The Blokehead Kids Series

We enjoy and welcome any feedback to make these series even more useful and entertaining for you.

INTRODUCTION

OneNote—is it just another pre-installed, memory-sapping program that Microsoft includes in its Windows OS? Many people do not even scroll through the different programs installed in their computers. Some think that OneNote is just another program pre-installed that they do not need yet they can't delete. Well, it's time to turn things around.

Today, discover how wonderful this app is and how valuable it can be for your everyday needs. Read this book to find out what OneNote is all about, what it can do and how to maximize its features.

Read on and learn.

CHAPTER 1
THE BEGINNER'S INTRODUCTION
TO ONENOTE

OneNote is one of the best innovations to Microsoft's Windows operating system. It's basically a digital app designed for note taking. Just imagine how one would take notes using the tradition pen and paper. Notes can be written anywhere on the page. Annotations, side note, highlights, even a few doodles are typical of a usual note. At times, a different colored pen is used to make these side notes or to highlight important parts of the note. This is also possible with OneNote. The notes made with this app highly resemble a note made with pen and paper- with all its jumbled information and all sorts of side notes and highlights – with all the convenience that the digital world can give.

Who will benefit from using OneNote?

People who take notes frequently can get the most benefit from using OneNote. These people include the following:

Students taking notes while in class while doing some research or while making term papers and/or projects. OneNote is also a great tool to use during group discussions or when discussing group projects. Planning parties, school events or activities for the school organization are also great reasons for students to use OneNote.

Teachers can use OneNote in organizing their lesson. They can also use it for their classroom and teaching needs like making notes on what topics to discuss, what needs to be re-discussed, what topics to go over, etc. Teachers would find so many uses for OneNote once they get the hang of using it. It allows for more versatility and more capabilities that can make a teacher's job so much more organized and files easy to retrieve.

Office work is so much more organized with OneNote. Say goodbye to misplaced files, tons of sticky notes, mountains of folders, and endless literal paper trails. Notes from several meetings will never be replaced. Important client calls or updates will always be up front and center. Any documents can be updated, annotated for changes, highlighted for critical parts, etc. Nothing gets lost in a mountain of files any more. Whenever one document or information is needed, finding it will no longer be a feat. A few taps and everything is readily available.

Events planners no longer have to carry numerous cards for florists, caterers, venue contacts, etc. They no longer have to keep separate files for each client, each contact, and each section of an event that has its own set of requirements. OneNote makes it so much easier to update needs, keep track of changes, or to make the necessary adjustments. It's so much easier, and delays and other "disasters" can be avoided.

Moms, whether working or full-time stay-at-home, can also use OneNote for various purposes. You can keep track of due dates of insurance or mortgages, or other payments, doctor's and dentist's appointments, car maintenance schedules, holidays, anniversaries, birthdays, events, get-togethers, and other important schedules of home and family life.

Practically anyone who has ever experienced dealing with paperwork, research, and information will understand how easily and how quickly these things can become so overwhelming. Fortunately, OneNote is one app that can help anyone get things organized. It is like an expanded planner that allows users to do so much more.

OneNote is not the only note-taking app available. There are several others out there but OneNote stands out as the leading app when it comes to helping improve productivity. OneNote places more focus on typed and handwritten notes, with capabilities for audio recording. Search tools allow users to bring up any file quickly, without having to waste time in opening several folders. The best unique feature is the smart integration of notes with the rest of the programs in Microsoft Office.

CHAPTER 2
ONENOTE DESIGN

The structure of OneNote is clearly defined and highly organized. It closely resembles the dynamics of physically taking down notes with a pen and paper. The entire app is like working with a physical, traditional notebook, with tabs and several pages. Just think of a thick notebook separated into smaller sections or "mini notebooks," and each mini notebook has a number of pages on which the users can write.

Basic Design

In OneNote, users can have multiple notebooks which are designated along the left side of the page. Tabs separate various portions of each notebook into sections. These tabs are located across the top of the notebooks. Each section holds pages where notes are made. The pages of the notes are listed along the right portion of the OneNote window. Nesting notes under another note is also possible, which further allows for better organization or for breaking up long lists.

This basic design is very effective in systematized breaking up of tasks like, for instance, planning and organizing several events, like an upcoming wedding, a birthday, and a community cookout all in the same week. That's a pretty hectic schedule and is a very huge challenge in staying organized and in accomplishing everything. This is also one opportunity to showcase how well OneNote keeps everything organized and on the right track. Each event is placed in one single notebook, with tabs for different elements like one tab for catering and food menu, another for venue details, another for guest list and their contact numbers, etc. With just one click, all the needed information are instantly accessible, easy to keep track of and easy to update.

There is also QuickNotes. This is a default tab where all new notes are automatically saved. For example, web clippings are instantly saved under QuickNotes. Taking a screen shot with the **Windows + N** shortcut also saves it under QuickNotes. Later, these notes can be saved under categories that are more specific.

OneNote Full Version

OneNote is available across several platforms. It can be used in iOs, Linux, and Android. Naturally, though, the full version with the best features is available on Windows. Full premium features, once available as paid version, is free with OneNote2013 for Windows.

Among the most notable unique OneNote capabilities are the following:

• Clip screenshots of maps online, which get automatically saved to OneNote. These screenshots can be edited, with specific instructions drawn on them to make them more meaningful and more helpful.

• Handwritten to text. This is a very cool feature that extends to the Math tool in Office. A user can handwrite a Math equation and OneNote converts it into text. It is helpful in the case of students in class taking down notes, frantically scribbling equations, or researchers and math geeks experiencing a "eureka" moment with an equation that might just change the world. This feature reduces the risk of mistaken inputs. Math equations are very tricky and a wrong letter, number, character, or mathematical operation can ruin the whole thing. Even a misplaced subscript or superscript, parentheses or equal sign is a disaster. Chemistry stuff also benefits a lot from this feature.

• Record and share the note. What better way to show off and be helpful at the same time other than record a lecture or a meeting, and then share it through a shared notebook with others who weren't able to get it or essentially got bored and slept through it.

• Embedding files from several Office program within OneNote is possible. For example, create a document from Word and an Excel spreadsheet. Both can be embedded and then edited in OneNote.

• Quick toggle between enterprise and personal accounts is another great feature. This is a great advantage for multitaskers as it ensures managing career and home at the same time with ease. OneNote saves and syncs them and still keeps them separate. This can be pretty convenient when needing to quickly grab some information from a personal account while working on something from work, or vice versa.

• For those using Windows Phone, OneNote is already pre-installed. This comes with a really cool new feature, the Office Lens. This is OneNote's sister app that allows users to snap pictures of notes, presentations, whiteboards, business cards, receipts or practically anything, instead of writing everything down. Then, any texts contained in those snapshots are automatically converted into a note, with full editing options as a Word document or PowerPoint file.

Mac Versions

Microsoft has recently released a OneNote version for Mac. This version has brought OneNote to the Mac desktop for the first time. It has a similar interface with the Windows version but its features are much fewer and the tabs across the notebook's upper portion are also fewer.

CHAPTER 3
A LOOK AT ONENOTE

To work with OneNote is much like working with a real notebook. You scribble along margins, highlight portions, draw arrows, paste cards, place some post-its, etc. To keep things more organized and easy to go back to, a notebook has tabs that separate pages into different sections. And for each section, there are pages. All these are possible digitally.

HACK #1: Special Keyboard Shortcuts

Keyboard shortcuts make working with OneNote much easier. The most helpful ones are:

• **CTRL + M**: Opens a new window in OneNote

• **CTRL + ALT + D**: Docks OneNote

• **CTRL + Shift + H**: any selected texts are highlighted

• **CTRL + K**: This allows for links to be inserted into the note

• **Enter** key: This opens the current link where the cursor is located

• **CTRL + Shift + C**: The format of the currently highlighted or selected text is copied.

• **CTRL + ALT + P**: This will start the playback of any selected video or audio.

• **CTRL + ALT + Y**: This will rewind or replay a currently playing audio or video a few seconds back.

• **CTRL + ALT + U**: This will play a video or audio a few second forward.

• **F11**: Allows toggled full screen views

• **CTRL + Shift + T**: Moves the cursor quickly to where the title of the page is.

• **CTRL + E**: This quickly accesses the search tool and searches all of the saved notes.

• **CTRL + Shift + E**: Selected pages are sent through e-mail.

• **CTRL + T**: This will create a new section within a notebook.

• **CTRL + Alt + M**: The current page is copied or moved.

• **CTRL + Alt + Shift + (Plus Sign)**: This zooms in the screen view.

• **CTRL + Alt + Shift + (Hyphen)**: Zooms out.

CHAPTER 4
WORKING WITH NOTES

Typing notes is no longer a boring, tedious activity in OneNote. There are more exciting ways to note taking than the usual typing. Here are a few tips to help you maximize the features of this app:

HACK #2: Audio and Video Notes

Spice up the usual note taking and use video and audio recordings as well. To do this, look at the **INSERT** option in the menu bar, at the uppermost section of the OneNote window, then follow these short, simple steps:

Step 1: A dropdown menu will appear.

Step 2: Choose the option **Record Audio/Record Video**.

Step 3: A video or audio recording will automatically start once step 2 is done.

Why Take Audio or Video Notes?

There are so many reasons for taking video and audio notes. First off, it's more convenient and less tedious than typing. This is very helpful for people who can't type fast enough to keep up with lectures, brainstorming sessions, meetings, etc. Also, detail-specific and critical sessions fare much better when notes are in video or audio forms. This way, fewer errors can be made in translating information and keeping copies of it for later perusal.

The pressure of having to take notes and concentrate on the moment may prove to be quite a challenge for some. Audio and video types of notes save so much time. One can concentrate on listening and understanding what is being said.

Notes look more interactive with the mix of different note types. Going back to these notebooks is more exciting and less boring. Instead of seeing a sea of texts, different file types make a note look more dynamic.

And best of all, people can just take a break from all the hard work of typing as fast as possible.

How to Retrieve Audio or Video Notes?

But wait. So, video and audio notes were recorded. How will these notes be retrieved? Would this mean opening each recording one by one just looking for that one note? Thankfully, it doesn't have to be that way as OneNote has an indexing feature to keep track of these note types. This feature allows for easy searching through notes to look for that needed video or audio file. To make these audio and video even more accessible and helpful, index them with these simple steps:

Step 1: Look for **File** menu in the menu bar (across the topmost portion of OneNote window).

Step 2: The menu appears. Select **Options**.

Step 3: The **Options** menu window appears. Choose **Audio & Video**, located at the options listed at the right portion of this **Options** window.

Step 4: At the Right side of this window, audio and video options will open. Look through it and find the checkbox next to the option "**Enable searching audio and video recordings for words**". This is often at the bottom portion.

Video and audio recordings are now automatically indexed once recording is done. This way, when typing search keywords, the words within these recordings are included in the search.

HACK #3: To Do Lists

OneNote is a great tool for organizing things, including activities. The To Do List option makes it easy to just type in activities. This feature eliminates the need in creating the checkboxes and other time-consuming formatting options to make it look like a physical, traditionally hand-written checklist of things to accomplish.

Step 1: Press the keys **CTRL** and **1** anywhere in the workspace of a page. A checkbox appears and start writing that To Do list.

Step 2: Type the activity.

Step 3: Press **Enter** key. Another checkbox appears, ready for the next item on the To Do list.

Step 4: To end the list, type in the last item and press Enter key. Then in this next line, press **CTRL 1** again to remove the last checkbox.

Now, every time an activity in this list is done, check the box. There are 2 ways to do this. One, simply position the cursor inside the checkbox and click on it. Two, bring the cursor to the item and press CTRL 1.

HACK #4: Page Templates

Page templates are not a very popular choice among OneNote users, but it offers so many benefits, especially when a user knows how to take advantage of these. There are academic templates that automatically provide a page very conducive for taking academic or lecture notes. These templates have predefined spaces for better organization of academic notes. For instance, there are already sections where the user can put notes such as topic for the day and important points covered. There is a title box at the top of the workspace where the user can enter the topic title or class name. Below the title box is an automatic entry of the day and tome when the new page was made.

There are also options for other common types of notes such as a blank page, and pages that cater to business note taking needs, decorative, and a planners' template.

To access the templates:

Step 1: Choose **Insert** from the Main Menu bar for newer OneNote versions. For older versions, choose **Format** from the Main Menu.

Step 2: A drop down menu appears. Select **Pages Template**. For older OneNote versions, choose **Templates** from the drop down menu.

Step 3: A panel opens at the right side of the page, listing the options for different templates. Simply click on the one that best suits the current note taking needs.

Creating a personalized page template is also possible:

Step 1: Create a new blank note.

Step 2: Format the note according to preferences.

Step 3: Once done with Step 2, click the **Insert** (for newer OneNote versions) or **Format** (for older OneNote versions such as OneNote 2007) from the Main Menu bar.

Step 4: Choose the option **Page Templates**.

Step 5: The pane for the **Template** menu opens. Find and click on the option "**Save Current Page as Template**".

Step 6: A dialog box opens. Enter the title for this customized page template.

Step 7: After details are entered, click the **Save** button.

Step 8: A new template category will appear in the Template pane, called "**My Templates**". The newly saved template will appear in this new category.

CHAPTER 5
BETTER NOTE MANAGEMENT

The best-selling point of OneNote is its high level for organizing notes. The app is meant for keeping things very organized and easy to retrieve. Organization of files is much like real-world organization of notes in the sense that separate notebooks are used for each subject or topic. Then, each main item of a topic is separated into sections. Various notes for each subtopic are written into the pages.

Beginners often create notebooks too sparingly. OneNote allows for quite a good number of notebooks and pages to suit every need. In fact, the more notebooks and sections created, the easier it is to search for files and notes later.

Filing and Organizing

OneNote filing and search system is very different from the rest of the Office. Having more folders results in a lot of things getting buried in sub folders within subfolders, making searching difficult. With OneNote, everything is easy to locate. All the notebooks are readily seen at the left side of the workspace. Tabs or sections of each notebook are across the top and the pages are at the left side. Every portion of a notebook or section is readily available. Just click on it and the note is instantly available. It's like flipping through an actual notebook with tabs guiding where to find a specific note.

One example of organizing stuff in various notebooks and sections in OneNote is illustrated as follows:

For a Personal Assistant in a business office:

Notebook	Section	Pages
MONDAY	AM appointments	• List of Clients • Meetings
	PM appointments	• List of clients • Meetings
OFFICE INVENTORY	Dental supplies	• List of supplies and how many • Contact numbers of suppliers
	Dental equipment	• List of equipment • Contact list for technicians, repair men or equipment suppliers
BILLS	Office rent	• Schedule of payments • Contact number of leaser • Repair needs • Contact info of repair person or building administrator • Copies of receipts

	Utilities	<ul><li>Schedule of payments</li><li>Copies of receipts</li></ul>

For an Events Planner

Notebooks	Sections	Pages
GENERAL EVENTS NEEDS	**Caterers**	<ul><li>List of caterers</li><li>Usual menu available for each caterer</li><li>List of bakers</li><li>Price ranges for menus</li></ul>
	Venue	<ul><li>List of local venues</li><li>Contact info for each venue</li><li>Price range</li><li>Venue capacity</li><li>Special needs for each venue</li></ul>
	Florists	<ul><li>List of florists</li></ul>

		• Specialty flowers • Price ranges
	Sound systems	• List of DJs, with contact info and fees • Contact info for sound system rentals, with fees for each sound system offers • List of bands, contact info and prices
	Decorations rentals	• Lighting and fixtures: Rentals and Sellers, technicians and installers • Candles: Sellers, contact for specialty or personalized candles • Tokens: Makers of pre-made and made-to-order tokens and other party favors
	Tables & Chair Rentals	• Contacts • Types of chairs and tables available e.g., who

		offers plastic tables and chairs, picnic tables and chairs, chaise, lounges, sofas, wooden, antique, etc.
CLIENTS	**Client A**	• Event details • Venue • Theme • etc
	Client B	• Event details • Venue • Theme • etc

Creating QuickNotes

A QuickNote can be made without having to open the entire OneNote window. For instance, this is helpful when one is in a hurry to create a note but has no time for contextualizing. A QuickNote is similar to a sticky note in the real world. You jot down information on a sticky note and then stick it later or copy it into the notebook.

Step 1: Press **WINDOWS** key and **N**.

Step 2: A "Send to OneNote dialog box will open.

Step 3: There will be 3 options available- "Screen Clipping", "Send to OneNote (D)" and "New Quick Note (N)". Pres the **N** key on the keyboard or use the cursor to click on the option "New Quick Note (N)".

Step 4: A new OneNote window will open. Just type the notes and it will be automatically saved in the Quick Notes section.

Afterwards, the user can always go back to this note by accessing the Quick Notes section and organize it into its more appropriate notebook, section and/or page.

Step 1: Open OneNote.

Step 2: At the right-side panel, look for the icon of 3 pages spread like a fan. This icon is for "Unfiled Notes". Click on this icon.

Step 3: Sections containing the notes written using the Quick Notes window are opened.

Step 4: Right click on the tab of the note to be organized.

Step 5: A drop menu appears. Choose **Move**.

Step 6: A new window appears, listing the different notebooks available on OneNote. Click on the desired notebook and/or section.

Step 7: If the Quick Note is to be saved in a new notebook or section, look for the button "**Create New Section Group**", located at the bottom portion of the window.

HACK #5: Protecting Notes with Passwords

Notes can be confidential. Using passwords to protect notes is useful in several occasions. For instance, when collaborating and sharing notes, you should password-protect it so that even though the notes are sent to others, only those who know the password can open them. Also, password-protected sections will reduce the likelihood of other people getting hold of information after the user logged off a shared computer. While abilities to access the same notebooks over several devices are possible, there is a risk that the same notebooks might be opened by other users. This is a particular concern when accessing synced notebooks over public computers or borrowing others' device.

In OneNote, passwords can be enabled for certain sections of a notebook but not an entire notebook. This can limit access to more sensitive and confidential sections but still allow others to some of the other sections of a shared notebook.

Step 1: Open a section of a notebook.

Step 2: Place the cursor over to the tab that designates that particular section.

Step 3: Right click on the section tab to be password-protected.

Step 4: A dropdown menu appears. Choose the option "**Password Protect this Section**".

Step 5: The pane for the Password Protection task will open, where password details will have to be typed. This opens over at the right side of the window. Find and click on the option "**Set Password**".

Step 6: A dialog box (**Password Protection**) opens.

Step 7: Input the password in the box "**Enter Password**".

Step 8: Confirm the password by entering it again in the box "**Confirm password**".

Step 9: Once done, click the button **OK**.

The section is now ready to be shared but can only be opened and read by the intended person who holds the password. How long a section remains open can be specified, too. There is also an option where the section immediately locks once another section is opened or as soon as OneNote is closed. Subsequent access to the protected section would now require a password.

When choosing a password, choose a strong one. Combine letters in uppercase and lowercase, along with numbers and symbols. Be unpredictable. Do not use easy-to-remember passwords like birthdays or anniversaries. Passwords should also be at least 8 characters. Pass phrases consisting of at least 14 characters afford better security.

Always remember the passwords used for OneNote. If forgotten, Microsoft does not offer any password recovery features.

Other things to remember when working with passwords in OneNote:

- Make sure to check the CAPS LOCK key on the keyboard when typing passwords because they are case-sensitive.

- Access is restricted to password-protected sections after a user-specified period of inactivity or after OneNote is closed.

- When using OneNote search, the password-protected section will not be included in the list. It can only become part of OneNote search if the section is unlocked before a search is made.

- Any note flags in the pages of a password-protected section will also not be available in note flag summaries. To include the protected section, unlock it first.

- Sections protected with passwords cannot be accessed during live sharing sessions, even if the notebook is available for other to see. Also, it cannot be accessed even if the section is already open in the user's own OneNote window. To allow others to see the password-protected section, unlock the section before joining live sharing sessions.

- Video and audio recordings cannot be protected with passwords.

Changing Passwords

To modify passwords:

Step 1: Click on the tab of the section whose password is to be modified.

Step 2: Click the **File** button on the Main Menu bar.

Step 3: From the drop down menu, choose "**Password Protect This Section**".

Step 4: The pane for **Password Protection** opens. Select "**Change Password**". If this option is not available, that means the particular section is not password-protected.

Step 5: A dialog box opens. In the box "**Old Password**", type the section's current password.

Step 6: Enter new password in the box "**Enter New Password**".

Step 7: Confirm the new password by re-typing it in the box "**Confirm Password**".

Step 8: Click the button "**OK**".

Removing passwords

To remove the password from a protected section:

Step 1: Click on the protected sections' tab.

Step 2: Select the **File** menu from the Main Menu bar.

Step 3: Select "**Password Protect this Section**".

Step 4: In the task pane that opens, select the option "**Remove Password**".

Step 5: A dialog box appears. Type the section's current password.

Step 6: Click the button "**OK**".

Locking all password-protected sections at once

Users have the option to lock every section protected by passwords simultaneously, to avoid having to go to each section and lock them individually:

Step 1: Click on the **File** menu in the Main Menu bar.

Step 2: Click the option "**Password Protect This Section**".

Step 3: Once the **Password Protection** pane appears, click the option "**Lock All**". (OR, just press the keyboard shortcut **CTRL+Alt+L**)

Setting Password Protection options

Once sections are unlocked, OneNote will keep these section unlocked for a period. How long these password-protection sections remain unlocked can be set by performing the following steps:

Step 1: Select **Tools** from the Main Menu.

Step 2: From the dropdown menu, select **Options**.

Step 3: A **Category** list opens. Select the option **Passwords**.

Step 4: Once the pane for passwords open, the following options can be used:

Lock password-protected sections after I have not worked in them for the following amount of time: This option is selected to specify how long before OneNote will automatically lock a password-protected section.

Lock password-protected sections as soon as I navigate away from them: This option locks the section right after the user is done working on it, i.e., as soon as the user closes the section/OneNote or opens another section/notebook.

Enable add-on applications to access password-protected sections when they are unlocked: This option allows other users access to the password-protected sections temporarily, only when this particular section is opened by the user/owner.

CHAPTER 6
USING OUTLOOK

Outlook is another cool feature in OneNote. This feature allows for a more complete recording of meetings or lectures by allowing the user to add details to notes right from the calendar entry.

Hack #6: Creating Outlook in OneNote

Outlook can be created as part of a note even without having to open this program. And the best part is that this particular appointment made in OneNote gets automatically added to Outlook. It will be visible immediately upon opening Outlook.

Step 1: Highlight the text that would be added to Outlook appointment. If adding an entire page, section or notebook, place the cursor over to its tab.

Step 2: Select the option **Tools** from the Main Menu bar.

Step 3: From the drop down menu, click "**Create Outlook Item**".

Step 4: From the expanded menu, click the option "**Create Outlook Appointment**".

Step 5: The appointment window will open. Enter information in the required fields.

Step 6: After all the important information are entered, click the button "**Save and Close**", located at the toolbar "**Standard**".

Creating Outlook Task

Tasks can be made for Outlook while working in OneNote:

Step 1:

Creating Outlook meeting requests in OneNote

Meetings can automatically be scheduled in Outlook without having to close OneNote. Think of making schedules during a meeting or a class while taking notes, or sending meeting invitations while continuously working with OneNote. For instance, while taking notes, it occurred that a meeting is needed, such as when organizing and updating a project saved in one of the notebooks. Create a meeting request and send it to the concerned people.

Step 1: Access the **Tools** bar from the Main Menu.

Step 2: Click the option "**Create Outlook Item**".

Step 3: Select the option "**Create Outlook Appointment**".

Step 4: The **Appointment** tab appears. Several fields would require specific information that can help the recipients understand what the meeting request is all about and a few other details.

Subject field: Type the description of the meeting, such as "Emergency meeting re Q3 financial report, Group meeting for Social Studies project," etc.

Location field: Type where the meeting is to be held, such as "Board room 2", "Room 34, Science building", etc.

Enter when the meeting starts and when it is expected to end.

Step 5: Click the option "**Invite Attendees**"

Step 6: In the box "**To**", type the name/s of those who should attend the meeting.

Step 7: Click the "**Send**" button.

The Blokehead

For this feature to work, Outlook must also be open.

Changing Outlook tasks in OneNote

Outlook tasks can automatically be updated and edited while still working in OneNote:

Step 1: Open pages in OneNote.

Step 2: Right-click on the Outlook task to be changed. The following options will open:

New Start Date: To change the Outlook task's start date

No Date: To remove the task's start date

Mark Complete: To mark selected task as finished or completed

Delete Outlook Task: To delete the highlighted task

Creating Outlook Contact while working in OneNote

Even if the Outlook window is closed, a task can be made while working on notes or sections in OneNote. The added contact will automatically be updated in Outlook.

Portions of notes can be included in the Outlook contact's body. Either a text or entire contents of a page or section can be added. If adding a text from a OneNote page, highlight it. If adding entire notebooks, sections or pages, within the note container, place the insertion point (cursor).

Step 1: Click the **Tools** menu from Main Menu bar.

Step 2: Select "**Create Outlook Item**".

Step 3: Select the option "**Create Outlook Contact**".

Step 4: The window for Outlook Contact will open.

Step 5: Enter the necessary information in the appropriate boxes.

Step 6: Click the button "**Save and Close**", located at **Standard** toolbar.

Adding Outlook to notes

Step 1: Look for the **Home** button in the Main Menu bar in the OneNote window.

Step 2: Select the option "**Meeting details**". A list of scheduled meetings for the day will open in a small window.

Step 3: Click on one of the meetings to open the particulars like the time, place, subject, participants, etc.

Step 4: Step 3 will automatically add all the meeting particulars to the opened note.

To get and paste the particulars of meetings either in the past or in the future:

Step 1: Open the drop down menu of the **Home** button.

Step 2: Select "**Choose meeting from Another Day**".

Step 3: Navigate through past and future scheduled meetings using the buttons "Previous Day" and "Next Day".

Hack #7: Creating Links

Linking sections of a note further helps in making the notes or entries more accessible. Imagine writing long notes and then having to scroll through various pages or through long sections of a page to search for one important piece of information.

To link to specific passages or paragraph:

Step 1: Select the text.

Step 2: Place the cursor over the highlighted text and right-click.

Step 3: From a drop down menu, click on the option **"Copy Link to Paragraph"**.

Step 4: Paste the link to the desired area.

This will display the first line of text contained in this link. To enable users to open the original page of the link:

Step 1: Right-click on the link.

Step 2: From the drop down menu, select the option **"Edit Link"**.

Step 3: A dialog box will open. Click on the **"Text to Display"** field and change the text. This will now enable users to bring up the original page where the linked paragraph is found.

CHAPTER 7
SYNCING AND USING ONENOTE
ACROSS SEVERAL GADGETS

Syncing levels up OneNote from just being merely a glorified Notepad. All notebooks and notes are synced to an online account. Save the notes and notebooks in the usual way and then sync it so that these will all be accessible and updated through all devices.

How Sync Works

OneNote can be used across multiple devices- desktops, laptops, tablets, smart phones. Save a note in one device and the same exact note can be retrieved and edited in another device. Look at this illustration:

8 AM: Opened OneNote in a PC at home and made a list of today's tasks- meetings all morning at the office, lunch with a client, and site inspection in the afternoon. Plus, files needed for the meetings are neatly filed in notebook sections designated for each meeting. One notebook solely dedicated to the day's client is already prepared. List of things to do and to check for during site inspection is also properly noted in a section.

8:30 AM: On the way to the office and the assistant called to inform that the first meeting of the day would need more files. These files are stored in another notebook in OneNote. So, while stuck in traffic, access OneNote on the smart phone and include the needed files into the notebook for the first meeting of the day.

9 AM: Arrived at the office and went straight to the meeting. All needed files are well prepared and organized, accessed through a laptop. Presentation went without any hitch. Notes were quickly added to the same notebook while listening to others' presentation and exchange among the participants. Check the meeting on the to-do list as already finished.

10 AM: Went through all the scheduled morning meetings.

11:30 AM: One of the contacts handling one of the details regarding a client project called that one of the items is no longer available. Called another contractor offering a similar item, confirmed availability. Noted the changes in the client's notebook through a smart phone.

12 Noon: Met the client. Accessed the OneNote notebook designated for all the details of the project for this particular client, using a tablet because laptop had drained batteries. Notes showed recent changes. Client made a few changes of his own, written straight into the tablet.

Rest of the afternoon: Used tablet to create notes about site inspection. Accident happened and tablet fell on a pool of mud. Totally wrecked and can no longer be salvaged.

7 PM: Got home. Reviewed the days notes on home PC, including notes on the client and site inspection, everything complete.

As you can see, there are many ways the same notebooks can be accessed via different devices. This is a great feature, especially with people working with devices in hazardous conditions. Accidents can happen and precious data can get instantly lost. It's always comforting to know that there is a backup that looks exactly the way the note looked during the last session. Sync also helps in continuous working on projects. This is also perfect for people who keep journals, whether it's a personal diary or a journal for scientific or social research. There's no need to tote large PC or laptops everywhere. There's no need to reach and boot a PC when there's always a smart phone close by to take needed notes. Any device with OneNote installed can do the job.

This feature also eliminates the need to lug all notes and devices everywhere. Memory sticks with large memory capacities

Hack #8: Sync

The most recent OneNote version is with Office 2013. This version prompts logging into SkyDrive, which is the cloud storage solution of Microsoft. Logging in automatically syncs notebooks saved in the currently opened device.

Aside from logging into SkyDrive, saving and syncing notebooks are also possible with Office 365 SharePoint. Syncing is also possible with DropBox, as long as the DropBox folder is selected when creating a new folder on a computer.

Syncing in OneNote 2013

Sync settings can be switched between manual and automatic. This option is available under "**Sync Options**". This can be accessed by:

Step 1: Open File menu in the Main Menu bar.

Step 2: Open the **Info** panel.

Step 3: Open **Sync Options**.

Step 4: A dialog panel opens, with the default setting at automatic. Modify as preferred. But to get the most of the sync feature, leave it at automatic settings.

Windows Live SkyDrive

This is the newest feature (available with OneNote 2010 and later) that secures syncing across multiple devices. The best thing about syncing with SkyDrive is that the notebooks can be accessed using devices that do not even have OneNote installed. That means practically anything, as long as it has an Internet connection.

Step 1: Create a Windows Live ID by visiting www.live.com. Register an account.

Step 2: Open a notebook in OneNote.

Step 3: Select **File** from the Main Menu bar.

Step 4: From the dropdown menu, click **"Share"**.

Step 5: Select the notebook to be saved.

Step 6: Select the option **"Web"**.

Step 7: From the dialog box that will come up on the screen, select the **"Sign In"** button.

Step 8: Enter information in the appropriate fields to allow log in into the Windows Live account.

Step 9: Once logged in, click on the SkyDrive folder where the notebook should be saved in.

Step 10: Click the button **"Share Notebook"**.

Once uploaded, the notebook can now be accessed from other devices, whether they have OneNote or not:

Step 1: Connect to the Internet, on other computers, tablets or other devices.

Step 2: Go to www.skydrive.com.

Step 3: Log into personal account using the Windows Live ID.

Step 4: Select the folder where the OneNote notebook was previously stored.

Step 5: Place the cursor over the notebook. Do not click on it. A pop-up menu appears that show several options.

Choose preferred options opened in Step 5. To be able to edit the notes, select the option **"Edit in browser"**. This will open the notebook right within the currently opened web browser. The notebook is now ready for viewing and editing within the browser. This removes the need to have OneNote installed in the device.

In case the device has OneNote installed, choose the option "**Open in OneNote**". The notebook is now ready for viewing and editing within the OneNote application installed in the device currently being used.

CHAPTER 8
TAGGING NOTES

Tagging is placing small icons next to the notes so that at one glance, the lines of typed words and numbers are readily identified. This can be very helpful because at times, notes can be long, with several different types of information all contained in a single page. For example:

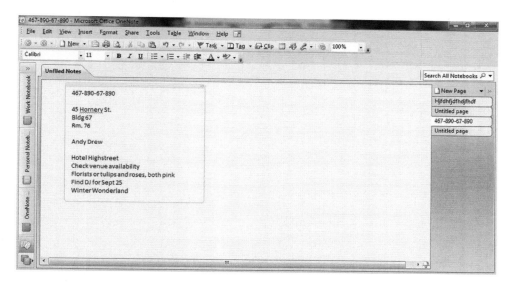

In the above example, notes may have been typed at a rapid pace, leaving no time to make certain headings and subheadings. Users can always go back and put icons beside these entries to signify what they stand for. Example:

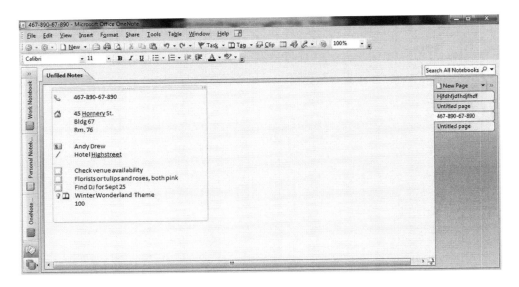

By adding tags, the entries make more sense. Also, the tags help to direct the user to a specific entry, eliminating the need to scan the entire note for the required information.

The above example only dealt with a short entry of information. Imagine if the note is already very long, filled with different information, such as when taking notes in a class. These tags can help break the text and make them much easier to read.

Content Tags

These are similar to tags one would place at the side of a notebook that physically separates the pages that belong to one specific section. This organizes everything for easy searches, better organization and quick access. The Content tags can be accessed through a drop menu in the Menu bar at the uppermost portion of the OneNote window.

Tags available in OneNote include the following:

To Do: Keyboard shortcut to create this tab is **CTRL + 1**. Using this tab will put 1 empty checkbox next to a particular entry within the note.

Important: The keyboard shortcut is **CTRL + 2**. Using this will put a yellow star adjacent to an item.

Question: Pressing the keyboard shortcut **CTRL + 3** places a purple question mark near a particular item. This can be used to mark items to denote an item that needs to be answered or confirmed.

Remember for Later: The keyboard shortcut is **CTRL + 4**. This will highlight items in yellow as a reminder that the item will be read or reviewed later.

Definition: The keyboard shortcut is **CTRL + 5**. This is used to highlight an item's definition in green.

Highlight: The keyboard shortcut is **CTRL + 6**. When using this content tab, a highlighter pen icon is placed beside a particular item.

Contact: The keyboard shortcut is **CTRL + 7**. This will put a contact icon adjacent to an item, which will designate an entry as contact information. This is more convenient than having to open a new file for contacts and then having to go back to a notebook again.

Address: Just like with the Contacts content tab, this one will place an icon of a house to denote a home or office address next to an entry. The keyboard shortcut is **CTRL + 8**

Phone number: This marks numerical entries as a phone number, with the hone icon next to it. Again, this saves time in having to open a new file to place contact information. The keyboard shortcut for this is **CTRL + 9**.

Website to visit: This icon denotes that an entry is a website or webpage to visit at a later time.

Idea: This light bulb icon can be used to denote that an entry is an idea to be pursued.

Password: This icon is a reminder that an entry is a password, but is highly discouraged. However, this icon may be used to denote that an entry requires a password.

Critical: This exclamation point in red is an icon placed next to items that are super important.

Project A and Project B: This icon is placed alongside entries that belong to specific categories or projects.

Movies to see: OneNote is not just for studies or for work; it's for leisure, too. For example, while talking to a client and then a movie title is mentioned as a theme for an event. Write the movie title down and place this icon. This can help as a reminder to watch or at least see what the movie is all about. Another example is during a lecture or meeting, a movie was mentioned during an icebreaker or as a reference. Write it down and mark it with this icon.

Book to read: This icon works similar to the "Movies to see".

Source for article: OneNote is equipped with everything that might come up during note-taking events. This includes when dong some research. This icon is placed alongside an entry tat denotes the source or reference.

Remember for blog: OneNote can be used in making drafts for blogs. This icon marks an entry to be posted on a blog.

Discuss with…: This icon content tab marks entries to remind the user of what specific topics or issues to talk to a person about.

Send in E-mail: this marks entries meant to be sent to someone through an email.

Schedule meeting: This icon reminds a user about a future meeting. Details can be added for better understanding, such as the name/s of those attending the meeting, when, where and the agenda.

Call back: This content tab marks an entry as a reminder to contact someone later, either with the contact details and/or with the issue to call someone about.

To Do Priority: This marks items according to priorities, as Priority 1, Priority 2, etc.

Client request: These mark items that were requested by clients.

Hack#9: Custom Tags

The latest version, OneNote 2013, allows users to create their own tags. OneNote is considered to have the most tags among other similar digital note-taking app. And this latest feature adds more tags to an already long roster.

Some of the most common and widely used custom tags in existence are:

Custom Tag	What It's For
$	Use this tag to indicate points that you think might make you some cash.
🖥	Tag note content to indicate PC content versus smartphone content.
📽	Tag note content that you want to pull out later for a PowerPoint presentation.
📱	Use this tag to call out content that is specifically for smartphone content as opposed to PC content.
🔭	Highlight note content that indicates you need to research it later.
📅	Tag content that you need to add to your calendar later.
🔑	Use this tag to call out key topics from lengthy notes so you can easily find the meat of the notes later.
❤	Tag note content that you just absolutely love and want to revisit later or share with others.
,,	Call out direct quotes without having to format them as such within the note. Also easily search for quotes.
☂	Use this to call out notes that are particularly problematic or, alternatively, use it to call out locations that are particularly wet and rainy, like Seattle.

CHAPTER 9
HACK #10: THE LATEST WITH ONENOTE 2013

Just like the rest of OneNote versions, users are given a clean, clutter-free workspace to type their notes. It's pretty much like a clean slate of paper, ready for note taking activities. All versions are practically the same, but with OneNote 2013, some features are improved and some new ones added.

Cloud

Cloud refers to file storage on the internet. Files saved here can be accessed at any time, as long as the user is online and has an account. SkyDrive is the cloud storage of OneNote. In OneNote 2013, cloud storage is called OneDrive.

New Note Taking Styles

Note taking in OneNote has become more like the physical, traditional note taking style. Users are now able to use stylus or their fingers to write on touch-capable devices like a slate PC, tablet or tablet PC- pretty much like writing on a piece of paper. Another good thing is that these handwritten notes can be converted into text. This is great sharing these notes and legibility is an important factor.

Captured Notes

In the latest version, the tool "**Send to OneNote**" is improved. Now, it is easier to clip an entire screen or portions of a screen. It is also now easier to send entire documents or Web page to a specific section in a notebook.

Embed Visio Diagrams and Excel Spreadsheets

Any type of Office file can be attached to any part of a OneNote note. This will store a copy of that particular file into the notebook. Excel spreadsheets are commonly created, whether to list down names, members, classes, finances, issues, items, etc. Create one directly on the OneNote page or, create one and then import it into OneNote notebook. The same is with Visio diagrams. Place these files anywhere on the OneNote page, where they are easily seen and conveniently accessible.

Better Tables

In OneNote 2013, creating tables is much easier and looks more sophisticated. OneNote table are no longer limited to drab, uninteresting flat tables consisting of plain lines. In the latest version, there are now more formatting options to choose from. Examples are choices for headers, data sorting within the cells of the table, and cell shading. This way, users can easily organize and make information available in more interesting presentations and form.

Collaboration

This is so much convenient when a team works on one project. Members can access the shared notebook anytime, anywhere. Then, once opened, they can input their ideas, findings and any other useful information into the notebook. Other members that have access to the shared notebook can automatically see these changes and input their own. Revisions and any changes in the notebooks are tracked and each change or addition is specifically identified with OneNote's integrated identity profiles. So, for example, the team leader checks the team's OneNote notebook, he/she can see who made some changes, who added something, what were these additions/changes and when were they made. It allows team members to work on the same file, with each activity tracked for reference.

Another great thing about the latest OneNote version is that while having meetings online, OneNote notebooks can be shared. The recipients can access these notes even if the devices they have do not have Office installed.

CONCLUSION

Thank you for purchasing this book.

OneNote does not need any special effort to download and use. It's readily available on Windows desktop as one of the pre-installed programs. Make use of it; start making note-taking a fun activity instead of a tedious, messy, and highly disorganized task.

Use OneNote now and organize your files—and your life—today.

Check Out Our Other Books

Self Help

ADHD Adult: How To Recognize & Cope With Adult ADHD In 30 Easy Steps

Conversation Skills: How To Talk To Anyone & Build Quick Rapport In 30 Steps

Ending Emotional Eating: Tips And Strategies To Stop Emotional Eating In 30 Days

House Cleaning Guide: 70+ Top Natural House Cleaning Hacks Exposed

Intuitive Eating: 30 Intuitive Eating Tips & Strategies For A Healthy Body & Mind Today!

Organized Mind: How To Excel In Math & Science In 30 Easy Steps

Organized Mind: How To Rewire Your Brain To Stop Bad Habits & Addiction In 30 Easy Steps

Organized Mind: How To Think Straight And Make All The Right Life Decisions In 30 Easy Steps

Stress Eating: How to Handle the Stress Triggers that Lead to Emotional Eating, Stress Eating and Binge Eating & Beat It Now!

Creative Confidence: How To Unleash Your Confidence & Easily Write 3000 Words Without Writer's Block Box Set

Creative Confidence: How To Unleash Your Confidence, Be Super Innovative & Design Your Life In 30 Days

Journaling: The Super Easy Five Minute Journaling Like A Pro Box Set

Journaling: The Super Easy Five Minute Basics To Journaling Like A Pro In 30 Days

397 Journaling Writing Prompts & Ideas: Your Secret Checklist To Journaling Like A Super Pro In Five Minutes

Habit Stacking: How To Set Smart Goals & Avoid Procrastination In 30 Easy Steps (Box Set)

Habit Stacking: Goal Setting: How To Set Smart Goals & Achieve All Of Them Now

Habit Stacking: How To Change Any Habit In 30 Days

Habit Stacking: How To Beat Procrastination In 30+ Easy Steps (The Power Habit Of A Go Getter)

Habit Stacking: How To Write 3000 Words & Avoid Writer's Block (The Power Habits Of A Great Writer)

Declutter Your Home Fast: Organization Ideas To Declutter & Organize Your Home In Just 15 Minutes A Day!

Emotional Vampires: How to Deal with Emotional Vampires & Break the Cycle of Manipulation. A Self Guide to Take Control of Your Life & Emotional Freedom

Memory Improvement: Techniques, Tricks & Exercises How To Train and Develop Your Brain In 30 Days

Mind Mapping: Step-By-Step Beginner's Guide In Creating Mind Maps!

Hobbies & Crafts

Doodling: How To Master Doodling In 6 Easy Steps

Making Costume Jewelry: An Easy & Complete Step By Step Guide

Paracord Bracelets & Projects: A Beginners Guide (Mastering Paracord Bracelets & Projects Now)

Jewelry Making For Beginners: A Complete & Easy Step by Step Guide

How To Make Jewelry With Beads: An Easy & Complete Step By Step Guide

Silver Jewelry Making: An Easy & Complete Step by Step Guide

Gaming & Entertainment

The Miner's Combat Handbook: 50+ Unofficial Minecraft Strategies For Combat Handbook Exposed

The Miner's Traps: 50+ Unofficial Minecraft Traps Exposed!

The Miner's XBOX 360 Handbook: 50+ Unofficial Minecraft XBOX 360 Tips & Tricks Exposed!

Miner's Kids Stories: Unofficial 2015 Box Set of 50+ Minecraft Short Stories, Jokes, Memes & More For Kids

Miner's Survival Handbook: Unofficial 2015 Box Set of Minecraft Cheats, Seeds, Redstone, Mods, House And More!

The Miner's Redstone 2015: Top Unofficial Minecraft Redstone Handbook Exposed!

The Miner's Seeds 2015: Top Unofficial Minecraft Seeds Tips & Tricks Handbook Exposed!

The Miner's Mod 2015 : Top Unofficial Minecraft Mods Tips & Tricks Handbook Exposed!

The Miner's Pocket Edition 2015: Top Unofficial Tips & Tricks Minecraft Handbook Exposed!

The Miner's Jokes For Kids : 50+ Unofficial Collection Of Minecraft Fun Jokes, Memes, Puns, Riddles & More!

The Miner's Craft 2015: Top Unofficial Minecraft Tips & Tricks Handbook Exposed!

The Miner's House 2015: Top Unofficial Minecraft House Tips & Handbook Exposed!

The Miner's A - Z Unofficial Compendium For Minecraft Combat Success

Kids Stories From The Miner: 50+ Unofficial Collection Of Fun Minecraft Stories Of Creepers, Skeleton & More For Kids

The Miner's Cheats 2015: Top Unofficial Minecraft Cheats Handbook Exposed!

Poker Strategy: How To Get The Unfair Winning Edge In Any Tournament. The Secret Strategies Of Poker Mega Stars Revealed!

Diet

10 Day Green Smoothie Cleanse: A Box Set of 100+ Recipes For A Healthier You Now!

10 Day Green Smoothie Cleanse: 50 New And Fat Burning Paleo Smoothie Recipes For Your Rapid Weight Loss Now

10 Day Green Smoothie Cleanse: 50 New Beauty Blast Recipes To A Sexy New You Now

10 Day Green Smoothie Cleanse: 50 New Cholesterol Crusher Recipes To Reduce Cholesterol The Natural Way

10 Day Green Smoothie Cleanse: 50 New Cholesterol Crusher Recipes To Reduce Cholesterol The Natural Way

10 Day Green Smoothie Cleanse: 50 New Sleep Helper Recipes Revealed! Get The Sleep You Deserved Now

Autoimmune Paleo Cookbook: Top 30 Autoimmune Paleo (AIP) Breakfast Recipes Revealed!

Dash Diet Plan: The Ultimate Dash Diet Cheat Sheet For Weight Loss

Dash Diet Recipes: Top DASH Diet Cookbook & Eating Plan For Weight Loss

Green Smoothie Weight Loss: 70 Green Smoothie Recipes For Diet, Quick Detox, Cleanse & To Lose Weight Now!

Paleo Diet For Beginners: Top 30 Paleo Snack Recipes Revealed!

Paleo Diet For Beginners: Top 40 Paleo Lunch Recipes Revealed!

Paleo Diet For Beginners: Top 30 Paleo Cookie Recipes Revealed!

Paleo Diet For Beginners: Top 30 Paleo Comfort Food Recipes Revealed!

Paleo Diet For Beginners: Top 30 Paleo Bread Recipes Revealed!

Paleo Diet For Beginners: 70 Top Paleo Diet For Athletes Exposed!

Paleo Diet For Beginners: Top 30 Paleo Pasta Recipes Revealed!

Paleo Diet For Beginners: Top 50 Paleo Smoothie Recipes Revealed!

Autoimmune Paleo Cookbook: Top 30 Autoimmune Paleo Recipes Revealed!

Paleo Diet For Beginners: A Box Set Of 100+ Gluten Free Recipes For A Healthier You Now!

Super Immunity Superfoods: Super Immunity Superfoods That Will Boost Your Body's Defences & Detox Your Body For Better Health Today!

The DASH Diet Box Set: A Collection of Dash Diet Recipes & Cheat Sheets

Health

Borderline Personality Disorder: 30+ Secrets How To Take Back Your Life When Dealing With BPD (A Self Help Guide)

Ebola Outbreak Survival Guide 2015: 5 Key Things You Need To Know About The Ebola Pandemic & Top 3 Preppers Survival Techniques They Don't Want You To Know

Thyroid Diet: Thyroid Solution Diet & Natural Treatment Book For Thyroid Problems & Hypothyroidism Revealed!

Bipolar Disorder: Am I Bipolar? How Bipolar Quiz & Tests Reveal The Answers

Bipolar Diet: How To Create The Right Bipolar Diet & Nutrition Plan- 4 Easy Steps Reveal How!

Bipolar Type 2: Creating The RIGHT Bipolar Diet & Nutritional Plan

Bipolar 2: Bipolar Survival Guide For Bipolar Type II: Are You At Risk? 9 Simple Tips To Deal With Bipolar Type II Today

Bipolar Teen: Bipolar Survival Guide For Teens: Is Your Teen At Risk? 15 Ways To Help & Cope With Your Bipolar Teen Today

Bipolar Child: Bipolar Survival Guide For Children: 7 Strategies To Help Your Children Cope With Bipolar Today

Anxiety and Depression: Stop!-Top Secrets To Beating Depression & Coping With Anxiety... Revealed! - Exclusive Edition

Anxiety And Phobia Workbook: 7 Self Help Ways How You Can Cure Them Now

7 Top Anxiety Management Techniques: How You Can Stop Anxiety And Release Stress Today

Depression Help: Stop! – 5 Top Secrets To Create A Depression Free Life... Finally Revealed – Exclusive Edition

Anxiety Workbook: Top 10 Powerful Steps How To Stop Your Anxiety Now... - Exclusive Edition

Depression Cure: The Depression Cure Formula: 7 Steps To Beat Depression Naturally Now – Exclusive Edition

Depression Workbook: A Complete & Quick 10 Steps Program To Beat Depression Now

Depression Self Help: 7 Quick Techniques To Stop Depression Today!

Hormone Balance: How To Reclaim Hormone Balance, Sex Drive, Sleep & Lose Weight Now

Fitness

Kettlebell: How To Perform Simple High Level Kettlebell Sculpting Moves Top 30 Express Kettlebell Workout Revealed!

Strength Training Diet & Nutrition: 7 Key Things To Create The Right Strength Training Diet Plan For You

Strength Training Machine: How To Stay Motivated At Strength Training With & Without A Strength Training Machine

Strength Training For Seniors: An Easy & Complete Step By Step Guide For You

Strength Training For Runners: The Best Forms Of Weight Training For Runners

Strength Training For Beginners: A Start Up Guide To Getting In Shape Easily Now!

The Ultimate Body Weight Workout: 50+ Advanced Body Weight Strength Training Exercises Exposed (Book One)

The Ultimate Body Weight Workout: 50+ Body Weight Strength Training For Women

The Ultimate Body Weight Workout: Top 10 Essential Body Weight Strength Training Equipments You MUST Have NOW

The Ultimate Body Weight Workout: Transform Your Body Using Your Own Body Weight

Survival & Outdoors

Preppers Guide: The Essential Prepper's Guide Box Set

Preppers Guide: The Essential Prepper's Guide & Handbook For Survival!

Self-Sufficiency: A Complete Guide For Family's Preparedness And Survival!

Bushcraft: 101 Bushcraft Survival Skill Box Set

Bushcraft: The Ultimate Bushcraft 101 Guide To Survive In The Wilderness Like A Pro

Bushcraft: 7 Top Tips Of Bushcraft Skills For Beginners

Religion

Religion For Atheists: The Ultimate Atheist Guide & Manual On The Religion Without God

Finance

Bitcoin: The Ultimate A-Z Of Profitable Bitcoin Trading & Mining Guide Exposed!

Minimalist: How To Prepare & Control Your Minimalist Budget In 30 Days Or Less & Get More Money Out Of Life Now

Cooking & Recipes

Kids Recipes Book: 70 Of The Best Ever Lunch Recipes That All Kids Will Eat… Revealed!

Kids Recipes Book: 70 Of The Best Ever Dinner Recipes That All Kids Will Eat… Revealed!

Kids Recipes: 70 Of The Best Ever Big Book Of Recipes That All Kids Love… Revealed!

Kids Recipes Books: 70 Of The Best Ever Breakfast Recipes That All Kids Will Eat… Revealed!

Barbecue Cookbook: 70 Time Tested Barbecue Meat Recipes Revealed!

Vegetarian Cookbooks: 70 Complete Vegan Recipes For Her Weight Loss & Diet Guide… Revealed!

Vegan Cookbook: 70 Vegan Breakfast Diet For Her Weight Loss Book… Revealed!

Vegan Cookbooks: 70 Scrumptious Vegan Dinner Recipes For Her Weight Loss... Revealed!

Vegan Cookbooks: 70 Vegan Lunch Recipes & Vegan Diet For Her Weight Loss Guide Revealed!

Barbecue Cookbook: 140 Of The Best Ever Barbecue Meat & BBQ Fish Recipes Book... Revealed!

BBQ Recipe: 70 Of The Best Ever Barbecue Vegetarian Recipes... Revealed!

BBQ Cookbooks: Make Your Summer Go With A Bang! A Simple Guide To Barbecuing

Barbecue Recipes: 70 Of The Best Ever Barbecue Fish Recipes... Revealed!

BBQ Recipe Book: 70 Of The Best Ever Healthy Barbecue Recipes... Revealed!

Barbecue Cookbook: 140 Of The Best Ever Healthy Vegetarian Barbecue Recipes Book... Revealed!

Grain Free Cookbook: Top 30 Brain Healthy, Grain & Gluten Free Recipes Exposed!

Technology

Scrum – Ultimate Guide To Scrum Agile Essential Practices!

Raspberry Pi: Raspberry Pi Guide On Python & Projects Programming In Easy Steps

Languages

Learn Languages: How To Learn Any Language Fast In Just 168 Hours (7 Days)

Pets

Essential Oils For Cats: Essential Oil Recipes, Usage, And Safety For Your Cat

Sports

Golf Instruction: How To Break 90 Consistently In 3 Easy Steps

Like Us On Facebook

https://www.facebook.com/theblokehead

PUBLISHERS NOTES

Disclaimer

This publication is intended to provide helpful and informative material. It is not intended to diagnose, treat, cure, or prevent any health problem or condition, nor is intended to replace the advice of a physician. No action should be taken solely on the contents of this book. Always consult your physician or qualified health-care professional on any matters regarding your health and before adopting any suggestions in this book or drawing inferences from it.

The author and publisher specifically disclaim all responsibility for any liability, loss or risk, personal or otherwise, which is incurred as a consequence, directly or indirectly, from the use or application of any contents of this book.

Any and all product names referenced within this book are the trademarks of their respective owners. None of these owners have sponsored, authorized, endorsed, or approved this book.

Always read all information provided by the manufacturers' product labels before using their products. The author and publisher are not responsible for claims made by manufacturers.

Paperback Edition

Manufactured in the United States of America

Yap Kee Chong

8345 NW 66 ST #B7885

Miami, FL 33166

Createspace

Copyright 2015

Get Notice of Our New Releases Here!

http://clika.pe/l/10263/27048/

Like Us On Facebook

https://www.facebook.com/theblokehead

Printed in Great Britain
by Amazon